Indeed, the grace of our Lord has been abundant, along with the faith and love that are in Christ Jesus.
1 Timothy 1:14

**The intent and
purpose of this volume is to
give you faith, hope and
inspiration. Hopefully it will help bring
peace and tranquility into your life. May
it be a reminder of God's love, guidance
and His many blessings.**

**Our publications help to support our work
for needy children in over 130 countries
around the world. Through our
programs, thousands of children are
fed, clothed, educated, sheltered
and given the opportunity to
live decent lives.**

Salesian Missions wishes to extend special thanks and gratitude to our generous poet friends and to the publishers who have given us permission to reprint material included in this book. Every effort has been made to give proper acknowledgments. Any omissions or errors are deeply regretted, and the publisher, upon notification, will be pleased to make the necessary corrections in subsequent editions.

Cover photo: ©DWPhoto/iStockphoto.com

First Edition Printed in the U.S.A. by Concord Litho Group, Concord, NH 03301.

Amazing Grace
from the
Salesian Collection

Compiled and Edited
by Jennifer Grimaldi

Illustrated by
Robert Van Steinburg, Russell Bushée,
Paul Scully, Frank Massa, Dorian Remine,
Terrie Meider, Maureen McCarthy,
and Bob Pantelone

Contents

The Walk

I don't know where the road will lead,
But in the Lord I'll trust.
O'er bumps and rocks and hollow spots,
Travel them, I must.
But sure as I keep focused
On my final destination,
I'll journey to the end with Him
Without a hesitation.
Whether short or long may be
That walk along the road,
He'll be right there beside me
To carry all my load.
So if I keep my eyes ahead,
With a smile upon my face,
I know I'll reach the journey's end
To that far better place.

Ruthmarie Brooks Silver

You are my rock and my
fortress; for Your name's
sake lead and guide me.
Psalm 31:4

His Hand in Mine

With His hand in mine,
I find comfort and peace,
For all my fears, to Him I release.
He is my strength, my joy, my all;
With His hand in mine,
There's no way I could fall.

With His hand in mine,
I am safe and secure.
For I feel His presence and His love so pure.
And I am drawn closer, closer still,
With His hand in mine,
To follow His will.

With His hand in mine,
Nothing ever goes wrong.
For He fills my heart with joyous song.
Songs of His praise and glory to bring.
With His hand in mine,
Forever I'll cling!

Lou Ella Cullipher

Give ear, listen humbly,
for the Lord speaks.
Jeremiah 13:15

God Speaks Through Me

God speaks through me;
To God I do belong.
God wants me to sing
And touch the world with song.

God leads through me
So people hear my prayer,
Asking for peace
In countries everywhere.

God's healing hand
Had set the captives free.
Miracles of God
Are always told by me.

Come and rejoice –
His wonders are so true.
God speaks through me
And also speaks through you.

Edna Massimilla

Sing to Him, sing His praise,
proclaim all His wondrous deeds.
1 Chronicles 16:9

Special Joys

I like to sometimes wander
Alongside country streams,
Then sit beneath an oak tree
And have some sweet daydreams…

I like to pick wild berries
Away off in a glen,
And catch melodic chirpings
Of a busy jenny wren…

12

I like to walk with bare feet
On duneland shifting sand,
While awed with scenic wonder
Of a panorama grand…

I like to skip white pebbles
Across a rippling creek,
And feel the Summer sunshine
So warm upon my cheek…

I like to smell the flowers
So fresh and wild in fields,
Then savor all the special joys
That Mother Nature yields.

Virginia Borman Grimmer

The Impossible Dream

You can be what you want to be;
Give Him your dream and you will see.
For miracles are meant for us,
For folk simple enough to trust.

Just hold the thought, in faith believe
And trust in God and you'll receive.
Pray on and then wait patiently;
Fulfillment of your dream you'll see.

Just know the answer's on the way
When to God you sincerely pray,
And if you'll let Him dwell within
The answer to your life He'll bring.

For God has put that hope in you,
Desire to be – desire to do.
Impossible as it may seem
With God you will fulfill your dream.

Helen Gleason

Grant what is in your heart,
fulfill your every plan.
Psalm 20:5

Interruptions

Life comes with interrupions
That change our ebb and flow,
When we stand at the crossroads
Not knowing where to go.
There are road blocks and detours
That change the path we trod,
And sometimes they are intended
To lead us back to God.

Often, daily interruptions
Bring a blessing our way,
Or some unexpected pleasure
Designed to make our day.
Sometimes God will clip our wings
So we don't fly too high,
And once we have been grounded,
We learn the reason why.

Sometimes God will interrupt us
To turn our lives around,
So that we might see His footprints
And walk on holy ground.
We sometimes miss life's danger signs
While rushing to and fro.
That's when God interrupts us
And shows us where to go.

Clay Harrison

17

Unseen Beauty

All around us is an unseen God.
He cares how we each may live.
He gives us chances to choose Him,
Chances to love and forgive.
Let us not waste a moment of time
To prove our love in return,
For He is the One who gives us our breath
And causes the world to turn.

Margaret Peterson

A Wish for You

May your skies be filled with sunshine
Each day your whole life through,
May health and happiness be yours
Day in and out anew.

May each rainbow that you seek to find
Not e'er be sought in vain,
May each cherished goal you have in sight
Be yours to have and gain.

May hopes and dreams that you possess
One day for you come true,
May God walk always by your side
And light the way for you.

Harold F. Mohn

Blessed be His glorious name
forever; may all the earth be
filled with the Lord's glory.
Amen and amen.
Psalm 72:19

He's a Friend
That Sticketh Closer

He's a friend that sticketh closer –
A shepherd, Savior, King.
Jesus Christ, God's Holy Son,
Of His great love we sing.

When shadows overwhelm us
And the sun has faded fast,
If your heart is heavy burdened,
On Him your troubles cast.

He's loyal, kind, and faithful
And hears your humblest cry,
Just look upward unto Heaven,
For Jesus is standing by.

Though the road is rough and rocky
And the meadows filled with briar,
Call out and plead for mercy –
Christ can lift you from the mire.

Follow in His precious footprints
For they won't lead you astray –
You can trust our blessed Savior
Because He will show the way.

He's a friend that sticketh closer –
Matters not if rich or poor,
Just give your heart to Jesus –
Our Lord, reigns forevermore.

Linda C. Grazulis

Another Day

Another day to know the love
Of family and friends,
Another day to make amends
Before life's journey ends,
Another day to realize
The joy that life can be,
Another day to thank the Lord
For blessings given me.

Catherine Janssen Irwin

*We thank You, God, we give
thanks; we call upon Your name,
declare Your wonderful deeds...*
Psalm 75:2

Love Should Blossom

So many loving words to give
To those with whom we work and live;
So many words heal and bless
Another's hurt or loneliness.

A friendly smile, a glad hello
Can cheer someone who's feeling low;
Or just a little thoughtful deed
Will help fulfill another's need.

So many things that we can do
To help another's day ring true;
So many ways to show we care –
Love should blossom everywhere.

Kay Hoffman

Show us, Lord, Your love;
grant us Your salvation.
Psalm 85:8

The Sheep
of God's Pasture

We're the sheep of God's pasture,
Alike in many ways;
As we trust in the Good Shepherd
And offer Him our praise.
Like sheep, we have gone astray
To see what we could see,
But the Shepherd sought and brought us
Back where we ought to be.

We're the sheep of God's pasture
Here in the promised land,
Led to the living waters
By His almighty hand.
We seek His face, His touch, His voice
When we're afraid at night,
And we praise Him in the morning
For sending us the light.

We're the sheep of His pasture
'Tho scattered now and then,
Each depending on the Shepherd
In a world of "Might have been."
He leads us down a righteous path
'Tho narrow is the way,
And welcomes home the wanderer
When we have gone astray.

Clay Harrison

He Knows You Best

Whenever life just seems unfair,
And things don't go your way,
Don't choose to shout and stomp about,
Instead, begin to pray.
For your heavenly Father wants to know
Everything you're concerned about,
Each trial and temptation,
Every worry and each doubt.
And when you've talked with Him awhile,
You'll find peace and rest,
No longer will circumstances matter,
For your Father knows you best.

Connie J. Kirby

Bits of Heaven

I watched a butterfly as it
Went thistle-stopping o'er
The meadow and I got a view
Of beauty evermore.
I saw some seagulls on their way
Elbowing in the breeze,
And glanced a bit of Heaven there
While resting… 'neath the trees.
I held a kitten on my lap
And listened to it purr;
I felt so close to Heaven that
My heart did in me stir.
I'm thankful for the little things
That we see day by day –
Those little bits of Heaven that
Are strewn along our way.

Luther Elvis Albright

An Autumn Day

The day all dawned in loveliness
The sky of brightest blue,
Held cotton clouds of purest white
To glorify it too.
The Autumn leaves were shining fair,
The colors warmed my heart,
And then I knew this precious day
Would thrill me from the start.

The sun arose far in the East,
A bit of Heaven blest,
The hilltops touched the sky above
More lovely than the rest,
And then a valley snug between
How wondrous was the sight,
Of Autumn leaves caught by the sun
In turbulent delight.

How happy was this Autumn day
With all its fun and laughter,
Somehow I knew would fill my heart
With joys forever after,
For God had sent an Autumn day
All warm and soft and fair,
And loaned it to the whole wide world
To have – to love – to share.

Garnett Ann Schultz

I *will praise You with all my heart, glorify Your name forever, Lord my God.*
Psalm 86:12

Let Me Serve

Bless all I do, this day, oh Lord,
Please, may each little task
Reflect the love I have for those
Who will some small favor, ask.
From irritations, keep me free,
Should something interrupt,
May not my hurry spoil the day
Or harsh words, peace disrupt.
I ask that every task performed
Be done with care to tell
Each person I may reach today...
I love them... and how well.

Anna Lee Edwards McAlpin

God's Love

The wind blows gently through the trees,
The breath of God's sweet love;
The sun is shining bright and warm
From Heaven high above.

The days are getting shorter
As Fall is drawing near;
Our Father starts His painting
Of the colors all so clear.

The red, the orange, the yellow
Begin showing on the trees,
So beautiful the colors,
As they drift upon the breeze.

His mighty hand controls His brush
Wherever He does go,
Making colors bold to see
Because He loves us so.

Lucille West

You will show me the path to life,
abounding joy in Your presence, the
delights at Your right hand forever.
Psalm 16:11

Lord, Lead the Way

I put my hand in Yours
And walk with You this day.
You know what lies ahead,
Lord, Jesus, lead the way.
Whatever You may choose,
I know it's best for me;
You see the obstacles
My blinded eyes can't see.
And when the day is done,
My thankful heart still sings.
I do not dread the thought
Of what tomorrow brings.

Without a care I rest
Safe in Your sweet embrace,
Throughout the darkest night
Until the morn I face.
I count each dawning day
As such a special gift.
No longer in despair
Through broken dreams I sift.
And with You by my side,
The future I don't fear.
With my hand clasped in Yours,
All worries disappear.

Regina Wiencek

*For Your name's sake, Lord,
give me life; in Your justice
lead me out of distress.*
Psalm 143:11

Each and Everyone!

We each have God's blessed guidance,
We're born with hearts of gold,
We each have love inside of us
And courage strong and bold.

We each have time to come and go,
We each have day and night,
We each have hope and dreams inside
And we each learn wrong from right.

We each have peace to show and live,
We each have time of rest,
God gave us all a beautiful start
To fill our lives with zest.

If we should fail along the way,
If goodness leaves our role,
We each are given the chance to pray
To justify our soul.

Dianne Cogar

34

Life in Christ

When living for Jesus
You meet Him in prayer
To ask for His guidance,
His mercy, and care.

You're close to the Savior
When love fills your soul
To make serving others
Your ultimate goal.

In Christ all are kindred,
Unbounded by race;
It's seeing His presence
In everyone's face.

It's spreading life's goodness
And sharing the pain,
And finding in giving
Both blessing and gain.

Amy C. Ellis

Say a Little Prayer

Say a little prayer in the morning,
Say a little prayer at night...
Throughout the day, take time to stop and pray,
And everything will be all right.
Give the Savior all of your burdens;
He will take them all away...
And then you will see how happy you shall be,
Because you took the time to pray.

Say a little prayer in the morning,
Say a little prayer at night...
You'll breeze right along, for life will be a song
If you but start the day off right...
And you'll have a wonderful blessing,
You'll receive it right away
From God up above, with mercy and His love,
Because you took the time to pray.

It's so sweet to know we can always go
To the blessed Lord in prayer...
Anytime of night, anytime of day,
Knowing that He's always there...
Nothing is too hard for our Savior...
He can drive all fear away...
For He is a Friend on whom we can depend
If only we will stop and pray.

Lou Ella Cullipher

Watching

God is watching over us
And we should pay attention.
He will grant us wisdom
Without any apprehension.

We're created in His image.
God made us to be whole.
He gave to us a conscience;
It is built into our soul.

God is so full of patience;
We know that God is love.
He is always faithful,
Such a blessing from above.

We're touched by His Spirit.
We worship Him and pray.
God is watching over us
Each hour of the day.

Edna Massimilla

The Four Seasons

Summer, Winter, Spring and Fall –
The Lord, God, made them all.

For Spring is the beginning
When things are made anew,
Followed by the summertime
With green grass and skies of blue.

Fall seems to slip right in
And steal the show away;
With trees aflame and Nature aglow,
The earth is in full array.

Winter enters with a fury
Bringing north winds that blow.
Then the fields of darkened brown
Are covered with glistening, white snow.

May the seasons that God gave us
Fill our hearts with simple pleasure,
While letting us keep their memories
In our hearts and minds forever.

Shirley Hile Powell

My Pathway

Help me, dear Jesus, to follow
Your footsteps the best that I can.
Sometimes I know I may tarry
Or wander away from Your plan.

Life offers many temptations
With so many pathways to take.
Give me the wisdom and foresight
In every decision I make.

Help me to turn from my ego;
Give me the strength to succeed.
Let me instead be Your vessel
To follow wherever You lead.

I may fall as I'm striving to meet You;
I may suffer in pain on the way.
But I know that I will be worthy
To meet You in Heaven one day.

Then help me, dear Jesus, and guide me;
I know I can't make it alone.
I need Your direction and blessings
As I'm seeking my way to Your throne.

Patience Allison Hartbauer

*Teach me to do Your will, for You
are my God. May Your kind spirit
guide me on ground that is level.*
Psalm 143:10

Our Purpose

Some simple words of tongue or pen
Reveal to us what might have been.
A chance passed by to help a friend
To make a difference in the end;
A friendly word or gentle touch
Can change an attitude so much.
So as we journey on life's road
Beside someone with a heavy load,
Let's find a way that we can share
And by our actions show we care.
And so fulfill our purpose here
As we journey on year to year.

Margaret M. Johnson

A Talk With God

I hope that You can hear me, Lord,
I need to talk to You,
To place my burdens at Your feet,
My courage to renew.

I need to ask You for advice
In choices I must make,
And plead for special guidance now…
'Cause there's so much at stake.

I beg for reassurance, Lord,
As duties I perform;
For strength to see me through the day
And weather any storm.

Lord, please hear my humble prayer;
In Your heart I'll abide.
And thank You for the confidence
These daily talks provide.

Angie Monnens

I cry aloud to God, cry
to God to hear me.
Psalm 77:2

43

In Gentleness and Beauty

I am up most every morning
And in time to greet the sun;
It's a welcome adoration
Shining down on everyone.
And I'm sure the clouds of Heaven
Rolling around up there in space,
Share the beauty of the sunrise
With a lovely, tinted face.

Notice how the coral colors
Seem to have a hint of gold,
All in lovely adoration –
It's a sight to see unfold.
All this beauty God created
Never costing us a cent,
Like the dawn of early morning
That is surely Heaven sent.
Then in gentleness and beauty
He will tuck the sun away,
Send the splendor of a sunset
To the ending of the day.
Let us thank Him for the wonders
He created far and wide,
And the little bit of Heaven
Spread across the countryside.

Katherine Smith Matheney

Sharing Gifts

Don't hesitate to use your gift,
For it's not yours to keep.
Far better would it be for you
To share, is my belief.

A gift received quite willingly
From someone whom you love
Is meant for your enjoyment, true,
But blessed by One above.

So if your gift is writing
Or painting lovely scenes,
Or if some music talent
Instilled in you has been...

Be sure to thank the Giver,
Take pleasure in the gift,
And then distribute portions
To those who need a lift.

The Giver takes joy in giving;
The receiver does, as well;
And when it's shared with others, too,
That gift will always dwell.

Ruthmarie Brooks Silver

The Sign

I asked God to give a sign
That help was on the way.
For in my hour of need,
I simply cried and prayed.
Then a songbird small
Sat upon my sill,
Nodding his tiny head
While I sat very still –
He trilled a merry sound,
A peaceful, happy note.
My eyes began to water,
My heart now in my throat.

He sang to me sweetly
My cares all disappeared –
My burden now was lightened,
My saddened heart now cheered.
I turned to wipe a tear
But he had flown away.
How was it he had chosen
To seek me out this day?
I closed my eyes and smiled,
I knew the answer then –
God had sent him here
To give me hope again.

Charlene Kaminski

Heal Us

Please heal us, precious Jesus.
Please heal each bewildered soul.
Cast out every fear, and dry every tear.
Just whisper the words, "Be whole."

For Thou hath made the crippled walk,
And made the blinded see.
The withered hand has been restored.
Now heal us, Lord, we plea.

We do recall that Thou did say,
"Just ask, and we will receive."
Oh, may our faith not waiver, we pray.
Thy words… we do believe.

Amazing grace – to us is given.
Let all anxious moments flee.
With Thy tender care, please hear our prayer.
Now, heal us, Lord, we plea.

Edna Massimilla

Be With Me

Lord, quiet down my restless soul
And lead me in Your way.
Take away my pain and dread,
Be with me through this day.

You are the only one who knows me
And loves me just the same,
You bore my pain upon the cross
And took away my shame.

How can I ever thank You
For all the love You've shown?
I'll lift high Your name in glory
And worship You alone.

Dona M. Maroney

The Little Thanks

It's little things we're thankful for
That prove the most worthwhile…
The little joys that life will lend
That bring the biggest smile,
A pleasant word when hearts are sad,
A friendly helping hand,
A kindly soul that offers praise
And tries to understand.
So often when we kneel in prayer
To thank God in our way,
We only mention worldly goods
In words of thanks we say…

Forgetting blessings we receive
Each day that life will send,
No mention made of hope and faith,
The blessings of a friend.
The little thanks should still be voiced
If God would hear our prayer,
A yesterday with mem'ries rich,
Tomorrow, shining fair,
However small they oft times seem
They're worth their weight in gold,
So in your every heartfelt prayer
Let little thanks be told.

Garnett Ann Schultz

God Can

I cannot mend a broken heart
But this I know, God can;
True peace will come if I walk on
By faith within God's plan.
I cannot find new life, new hope
Through my own weak design;
But these will come at last if I
Live by God's will, not mine.

Phyllis C. Michael

I Trust in Thee

I trust in Thee, oh Lord, my God
Who meets my every need.
And oftentimes when anxious
'Tis Thee to whom I plead.

Thee alone can give me peace
And make the wrong seem right;
Who comforts me when weary,
Turning darkness into light.

Without this trust in Thee, oh Lord,
All things would seem in vain.
But I can face tomorrow
With Thy hand upon the reign.

Helen Parker

*I trust in Your faithfulness. Grant
my heart joy in Your help, that I
may sing of the Lord, "How good
our God has been to me!"*
Psalm 13:6

*He chose us in Him,
before the foundation of the
world, to be holy and without
blemish before Him.*
Ephesians 1:4

His Voice

Happily I'd choose to be
Up high upon the glassy sea
Of lovely clouds now passing by
Against a soft blue morning sky,
Like a procession straight away
With colors white and blue and gray.
Just watching them so full and grand
Makes me recall another land
When young and tender lying still
So long ago, a grassy hill;
I watched the clouds a long time there,
Then soft, a voice, I thought to hear
That seemed to say "I love you so,
My love will never let you go."
It seemed to hold me in its power,
So strange, yet wonderful that hour.
By grace that voice I've come to know;
It was my Lord so long ago.
One day to Him I'll fly away,
'Til then within my heart He'll stay.

Karen M. Wood

Deep Within

Deep within an acorn,
Is a graceful oak tree
Just waiting to be born,
For everyone to see.
Deep within an oyster,
A rare pearl lies concealed,
Until someone finds it,
Its beauty then revealed.
Deep within every heart,
There is an empty place,
That only God can fill
With His love and grace.

Steven Michael Schumacher

*I will praise You, Lord, with
all my heart; I will declare
all Your wondrous deeds.*
Psalm 9:2

May He grant you joy of heart and may peace abide among you.
Sirach 50:23

Joys of a Summer Day

A peaceful Sunday afternoon,
The whole earth seems to rest.
A weathered bench, a shady tree,
What more could I request?
While lingering by the water's edge,
Watching the fish swim by,
Reflected on the placid pond
Are trees, and clouds, the sky.
Birds sing sweetly, crickets call;
I hear the restless breeze
Whispering in the cottonwood,
A tune that's sure to please.
I love this place, this quietude,
To which I oft retreat.
It's here amidst God's handiwork
Where peace and beauty meet.
Forgotten is the troubled world,
There's only God and I;
And flowers, trees and trembling leaves
Beneath a sunny sky.

Regina Wiencek

In all your ways be mindful of Him, and He will make straight your paths.
Proverbs 3:6

Gentle Master

I will ask of the dear Master
To go with me through the day,
Be my constant guide and keeper
As I walk the narrow way.

I will ask He be my pilot
Or the captain of my ship,
Guide me safely to the harbor
As I journey on my trip.

Gentle Master, be my keeper,
Guide me safely to the shore,
Help me walk the straight and narrow
On my journey ever more.

Katherine Smith Matheney

But the wisdom from above is first of all
pure, then peaceable, gentle, compliant,
full of mercy and good fruits, without
inconstancy or insincerity.
James 3:17

And above all things have fervent love for one another.
1 Peter 4:8

Increase My Love for Others

Increase my love for others, Lord;
Oh hear my earnest prayer!
May I be sensitive to pain,
And truly love and care.

Broaden my smile, dear Lord;
May I more fervent be,
Going willingly out of my way
A lonely heart to see.

And let my greeting be warm and true,
Lovingly meeting the eyes;
Let no one go from my presence today
With lonely tears or sighs.

May I be quick to share my time
With anyone having a need;
May Christ be filling my heart today,
And be glorified indeed!

Helen Neimy

Life's Harvest

Life's springtime was a happy time
When days were warm and bright,
Life all abloom with pleasant hours
And not a care in sight;
The roses grew along the way
Each bud so fair and sweet,
The raindrops only fell it seemed
To make our dream complete.

Life's Summer hurried on its way
But still life brought a smile,
The seeds we planted blossomed forth
And all was worth the while;
Each dawn a treasure to behold
With something new and real,
Each afternoon of sparkling bliss
So pleasantly ideal.

But now life's Autumn near at hand
Has so much more to lend,
For seeds of kindness we have sown
We're harvesting a friend;
Though silver shows a tiny trace
We've mem'ries to recall,
And with the joy of springtime gone
We've found the gold of Fall.

October just a step away
The twilight drawing near,
We're harvesting the smiles and joys
We worked for through the year;
Life's harvest so abundant now,
The rich reward we've sought,
The Autumn's gold is blessing us
With quite a precious lot.

Garnett Ann Schultz

*Light is sweet! and it is pleasant
for the eyes to see the sun.*
Ecclesiastes 11:7

God's Heavenly World

They say God's world is a wondrous place
Filled with love and heavenly grace,
Where angels with celestial joy
Proclaim His word, and all enjoy
Enduring peace and brotherhood;
Where life's past trials are understood,
And each of us, with sins erased,
Shall reap the joys of God's sweet grace.

Vi B. Chevalier

Let Your Smile Shine Through

It is easy to smile when the sailing is smooth
And you're riding the crest of the waves;
When the world is your oyster, its pearl, shiny and bright,
It is easy to smile and give praise.
But, oh, let a storm on the horizon appear,
How then is your countenance, my friend?
Do you frown 'cause it's tough? Is your faith strong enough?
Can you smile if you lose in the end?
It's easy to smile when good fortune's your ship
And Lady Luck is charting the way,
The smile that takes courage is the one that shines through
When dark clouds descend on your day.

Kay Hoffman

The Lord let His face
shine upon you, and be
gracious to you!
Numbers 6:25

The Little Chapel in the Dell

The bells were softly pealing
In the chapel in the dell,
Their message, "Come and worship,
God is with us, all is well."
I heard the organ playing
As I watched the candles glow,
The choir thus was singing,
"Jesus loves me this I know."
My heart was heavy laden
As my soul was stained with sin,
'Twas then I prayed for courage
So that I might enter in.
Someone then came to greet me,
Yes, as I walked through the door,
I felt a peace within me
Like I'd never known before.

I heard the preacher's message
Of the cross and Calvary,
God sent His Son to save us,
Thus, He died to set man free.
The alter call was given
And I wondered, should I go?
I heard His still voice whisper,
"Come unto Me, I love you so."
I'm glad I heard that message
In the chapel in the dell,
No longer am I laden,
God is with me, all is well.

Mary E. Herrington

Nearby

His is a peace that I know best
When I'm attuned to Him;
Or when my problems seem to mount,
Or when my hopes grow dim;
When I've strayed and come back home
To find my prospects slim;
I only have to speak His name –
And nearby I find Him.

Henry W. Gurley

I Put My Cares Away Today

I put my cares away today
And said a little prayer,
That God would help me find my way
And deliver me from despair.
The golden sun came out to play
And filled me full of hope,
My burden seemed to fly away
And I began to cope.
I put my cares away today
As a rainbow came in sight,
And at the rainbow's end I found
My cares had taken flight.

Nora M. Bozeman

*Blessed is the man who
trusts in the Lord, whose
hope is the Lord.*
Jeremiah 17:7

One Day at a Time

I dare not fear the future,
Nor question Him who leads;
He who holds the stars in place,
The tiny sparrow feeds.

Today is here, how may we know
What another day may bring?
While skies are blue and all is well,
I'll trust and laugh and sing.

And when again the sun shall set,
And another morning dawns,
All is well, for today is here,
Yesterday's past and gone.

And if the storm clouds gather,
And then comes down the rain,
I'll look for a beautiful rainbow,
And the sun will shine again.

One day at a time, how swiftly they fly,
But I need not fear nor dread.
He who feeds the sparrow,
Knows what lies ahead.

His loving arms enfold me,
And He whispers, "Peace, be still."
He'll quiet the storm on life's dark sea,
The waves obey His will.

Helen Humbarger

I call upon You; answer me,
O God. Turn Your ear to
me; hear my prayer.
Psalm 17:6

I Hear His Voice

I hear His voice in the ocean's roar,
In the Winter wind and the rain.
I catch the whisper of sound at night
As trees tap my windowpane.

When I walk in the hills I hear His song
In the notes of a meadowlark.
By my fire at night on a cozy hearth
I hear Him again in the dark.

As embers flame and smoke goes up
In spirals to meet the sky,
I know He is there in my comfortable warmth
Though perhaps I hear only a sigh.

Wherever I go, wherever I am,
Be it mountains, the valleys or sea –
His music fills my listening heart
And I'm glad He is here with me!

Jean Conder Soule

*When you hearken to the voice of the
Lord, your God, all these blessings will
come upon you and overwhelm you.*
Deuteronomy 28:2

I Thank You

I thank you dearest friend of mine
For all the love you've shown,
For helpfulness and tender thoughts,
The laughter we have known;
The outstretched hand that's always there
Through days of strain or stress,
No matter what I say or do
You never love me less.

I thank you for so many things,
The pure delight we share,
The many times you'd stop to chat
And just because you care;
The words of praise that mean so much,
The hopes and smiles you lend,
Because you always take the time
To love me as a friend.

For every yesterday so sweet,
Tomorrows yet to be,
The moments rich in precious dreams
That mean the world to me;
For being you and loving me
Each day that God shall send,
My heart knows peace because of you –
I thank you, dearest friend.

Garnett Ann Schultz

A *faithful friend is
beyond price, no sum
can balance his worth.*
Sirach 6:15

Darling Children

Sunshine beams and snowy dreams –
Winter's on its way.
Children making snowmen,
Laughing as they play.

Cold air brushing rosy cheeks,
Sledding down the hill.
Jumping, screaming in the snow,
Oh Lord, what a thrill.

Bless these darling children
So full of dreams and awe,
And send Your heavenly angels
To protect them one and all.

Dona M. Maroney

Big Snow

White ermine cloaks
A sun splashed world
This brilliant, Winter day;
Bare limbs are draped
In snowy shawls
That catch each golden ray.

Soft, sculptured drifts
Line windswept roads
In flowing, classic lines;
Revealing in delicate beauty
The Maker's planned design.

Lola Neff Merritt

Grant what is in your heart,
fulfill your every plan.
Psalm 20:5

My Home

My home is like a citadel
Where malice cannot enter;
A fortress built on love and trust
Where God is in the center.

My fortress is not built of stone;
It is void of worldly things,
But it is rich in tolerance
That exceeds the wealth of kings.

Kindness fills the atmosphere,
Patience engulfs the halls,
And smiling faces… evidence
God dwells within these walls.

There is no space for anger here,
No place for gloom and doom,
For faith prevails and it reflects
God's love in every room.

My home endures despite the wrath
That life sometimes can dole,
Because it's held together with
The strength of God's control.

Patience Allison Hartbauer

Give to Him Your Cares

Give to God your worries,
And, yes, give to Him your cares;
For He is in control, you know
Your burdens He will bear.
Trust you're in His hands
And He'll not let you slip or fall;
Trust He'll do what's best
When it's upon Him you do call,
A sweet release and inner-peace
God offers these each day;
If only we would reach out
To Him and simply pray.

Gina Mazzullo Laurin

Troubled Heart

When your heart is troubled
And no one seems to care,
Don't believe it for a moment,
For God is always there.

If trouble gets you down
And life does seem so bleak,
Lift your eyes to Heaven.
The face of God now seek.

In your soul you'll know Him
And peace will fill your heart,
If you believe in Him
And try to do your part.

He never will forsake you –
That's a promise He has made.
Lift your heart this very day,
Then watch your troubles fade.

Bernice Laux

*For then you shall delight in the
Almighty and you shall lift up
your face toward God.*
Job 22:26

The Confession

My God, it makes me so ashamed
To fail You like I do,
When in my heart I truly know
I have no friend like You.

When I awake each morning,
Your love is always there,
Within the fragrance of the flowers
That blossom everywhere.

It matters not that I am weak
And cannot find the way;
The radiance from Your holy face
Will turn the night to day.

The sorrow, grief and pain I feel,
You always seem to share.
My heart is never heavy, Lord,
For it is in Your care.

My mind, my soul, my heart, my all
I'd give to You, gladly;
For I would staunchly live for You
Who freely died for me.

Myrtle L. Johnson

A New Day

Here it is a grand new day –
I have a fresh new start.
My slate is clean awaiting
The day's events to chart.

I hope I'll use the hours
Of this day in a grateful way,
Trying to be reverent
In all I do and say.

Each day's a great adventure,
A time to start anew,
To think about our motives,
If they be kind and true.

Then to show compassion
And help another's need,
Being Christian in our journey
In thought and word and deed.

Virginia Borman Grimmer

*Yours the day and Yours
the night; You set the
moon and sun in place.*
Psalm 74:16

God's Loving Hands

The beauty of the daffodils
In beds of snowy white;
The patter of a gentle rain,
A song of sheer delight.

The freshness of the ocean breeze
As it sweeps across the land;
Can there be doubt this would exist
Without God's loving hand?

The song of a canary
With such a pleasant tune;
The wondrous smell of springtime
With fields that are in bloom.

The birds that soar up in the sky,
All creatures on this land;
No doubt that this could ever be
Without God's loving hand.

So, thank Him without measure
For His blessings showered down,
That fill our lives with pleasure
'Til at last, we're homeward bound.

Albert N. Theel

Sing praise, play music; proclaim
all His wondrous deeds!
Psalm 105:2

God's Miracle of Spring

Wrens and robins back once more,
Hyacinths blooming by the door,
Lilac blossoms bending low,
Bright tulips blend in rainbow row.

Purple pansies with saucy faces
Peeping out from garden spaces,
Lemon lilies from buds unfold
To shimmer in shining purest gold.

Sun-jeweled bees for fragrance chose
The treasure of each velvet rose,
Our wondrous God in glory brings
His fresh, green miracle of spring.

Elisabeth Weaver Winstead

*How numerous, O Lord, my
God, You have made Your
wondrous deeds! And in Your
plans for us there is none to
equal You. Should I wish to
declare or tell them, too many
are they to recount.*
Psalm 40:6

A Loving God

I'm thankful for a loving God
To whom my heart belongs.
He's always there to forgive me,
If perhaps I should do wrong.

His love flows like a river.
It touches you and me.
Nothing does it cost us;
It's His gift to us, you see.

To know that I am safe and secure
In the arms of a loving God,
Is all the comfort that I need,
While I walk this earthly sod.

He always gently lifts me up
When I am sad or weak.
He is my life's salvation,
The One I love and seek.

Who else but a loving God
Could look at sinful me,
Then give His life in sacrifice
To set this sinner free?

Shirley Hile Powell

But may all who seek You rejoice and be
glad in You. May those who long for
Your help always say, "God be glorified!"
Psalm 70:5

My Sanctuary

My Sanctuary's anywhere
That I can kneel and pray,
For it may be a mountaintop
Or somewhere far away,
Or maybe just a humble spot
Within my own back yard.
My Sanctuary's anywhere
That I can talk to God.

Katherine Smith Matheney

My Bit of Paradise

There is a place that's set apart
From the local scene,
A little bit of paradise
Is what it really seems –
Where the sun's a little brighter
And sweet perfume fills the air,
From ever-blooming flowers
That enjoy their presence there –
Where the birds sing even sweeter,
And the butterflies that fly
Excel in vibrant splendor
That the eye cannot deny.
God knows, I feel not worthy
To call this acre mine,
For He's graced it with His beauty
And His blessings so divine.

Catherine Janssen Irwin

*Grace to you and peace
from God our Father and
the Lord Jesus Christ.*
1 Corinthians 1:3

Where There Is Faith

Where there is faith, hope abounds
And we can carry on,
Because we somehow learn to cope
While facing the unknown.
The future may have pitfalls
And snares that bring us down,
But faith is the umbrella
That will not let us drown.
Faith is more than just a feeling;
It's true belief in God,
Just knowing He will guide us
Wherever we may trod.
Faith is knowing prayers are answered
According to His will,
And that quiet voice within us
When all is calm and still.

Faith is sharing things with others
Who have a greater need,
And asking God to bless the gift
And multiply the seed.
How do they cope who have no hope
And they are all alone?
Where there is faith, hope abounds
And we can carry on!

Clay Harrison

Look, then: I will give them knowledge; this time I will leave them in no doubt of My strength and My power: they shall know that My name is Lord.

Jeremiah 16:21

Have You Taken It to Jesus?

Have you taken it to Jesus...
Have you gone to Him in prayer
With that problem that besets you?
Have you left it in His care?

Are you trusting Him completely,
Knowing He will work things out
For the best and in His own time?
Is your heart free from all doubt?

Have you yielded in surrender
At our precious Savior's feet,
And found there in sweet submission
Perfect peace and joy complete?

What a refuge there is in Jesus,
Just to cast on Him all care,
And to find our burdens lifted
At the blessed throne of prayer.

Beverly J. Anderson

*Then all who take refuge in
You will be glad and forever
shout for joy. Protect them
that You may be the joy of
those who love Your name.*
Psalm 5:12

The Word of the Lord

The word of the Lord is perfect,
And happy are they that hear;
It storeth the heart with knowledge
That shines like the noonday clear,
The word of the Lord is perfect;
The word of the Lord is pure;
And they, who in faith receive it,
Have anchored their hope secure.
The word of the Lord is perfect,
And thus it converts the soul;
The numberless worlds created
Are under its vast control.

The word of the Lord is mighty;
Forever its truth shall stand;
It speaks, and the winds and waters
Are stilled at its high command.
The word of the Lord is earnest,
Admitting of no delay;
It counsels, persuades, and urges
To come and be saved today.
The word of the Lord is precious;
The word of the Lord is love;
It tells of a life through Jesus,
A home and a rest above.

Fanny Crosby

The Innocent and the Blessed

When a child speaks to God,
They may ask for simple things,
Like to hear a lovely bluebird
Just the way it always sings.
Their thoughts are undeniably
So innocent and blessed;
Their hearts are made of precious gold
That shines above the rest!
They look into the heavens
With a smile upon their face,
Intrusting that the Lord will
Award the wish they place.
And as they pray for things to come,
Or loved ones they hold dear –
You can rest assured that from their hearts
These thoughts are most sincere!
For, God's children are pure and innocent;
They're His seeds of sweet delight…
And they long for love and meaning
To give it back with all their might!

Dianne Cogar

*May You be blessed by
the Lord, who made
Heaven and earth.*
Psalm 115:15

1-800-Heaven

The call is always ready,
It's never out of date –
Nor is it ever busy
Where you must sit and wait.

For Heaven's line is always open,
And God's forever waiting –
In view of all your special needs,
He's always contemplating.

You'll never be a number,
And you'll never be on hold –
Nor will you ever be upset
Or left out in the cold.

For God is always listening,
His line's direct to you…
He's with you every step each day;
He hears your heart speak, too!

Now the only charge you'll ever get,
Though there's no funds to pay –
Is giving God the same respect
And the love He gives away!

Dianne Cogar

> *You, Lord, are near to all who call upon You, to all who call upon You in truth.*
> **Psalm 145:18**

He's Always There

God's close to me
And always there…
My every pain
And joy to share.

He's nigh to me
Both night and day…
To lead me safely
Lest I stray.

I lean on Him
When in despair…
He marks my path
And shows me where.

I'm not alone
For He is near.
He helps me banish
Doubts and fear.

God's love and care
Are always there…
And closest when
I turn to prayer.

Amy C. Ellis

A Burden for a Song

I came to Jesus sore distressed,
Oh, how my heart did ache;
I could no longer bear my cross,
The pain, no longer take.

He said, "Child, lay your burden down
And place your cross on Me;
You've carried it so long alone,
My child, could you not see…

That all you needed was to ask?
My help is ever near.
To those who seek, I'll comfort, bless,
And free their hearts from fear.

I know the weary road you trod,
How bleak and dark the way;
Just trust Me now to lead you through
Into a brighter day."

I cried aloud, "Lord, please forgive,
I should have understood
That You who loveth more than all
Would work things out for good."

I then cast all my weaknesses
On Him, divinely strong;
Exchanged the burden which I bore
For peace, and hope, and song!

Beverly J. Anderson

In His Care

Why be so anxious
As we start a new day,
When God goes before us
To show us the way?
Why feel that dread
As it creeps up inside?
The Lord made a promise
He'd be by our side.
Why all the doubts
In our hearts and our minds,
When God our protector
Walks closely behind?
Before us, beside us,
Behind us, it's true –
Our God's all around
In all that we do.

Gina Mazzullo Laurin

With You

It's been said, "Let go and let God,"
And these very words are true.
If only you would believe
He'll always be with you.

He'll never let you suffer
More than you can bear
And you can always rely on Him
To always meet you there.

He'll be there in the hard times
And happy days too.
Remember His awesome love
Is right there with you.

Dona M. Maroney

Peace I leave with you; My
peace I give to you. Not as
the world gives do I give it to
you. Do not let your hearts
be troubled or afraid.
John 14:27

Success

Success is not a destination,
But a journey day by day
As we overcome the hurdles
We encounter on the way.
It's a lifelong work in progress
With pit stops here and there,
And before the journey's over,
We will need some repair.
Our attitudes dictate the path
We follow through the years,
For success requires commitment,
Even blood, sweat and tears.
Though many look for shortcuts,
Very few are found,
For when heads are in the air,
Feet aren't on the ground.

Success is an achievement
Which reaps its own reward,
Especially for those whose lives
Bring glory to the Lord!
Success creates a state of mind
Wherever we may roam,
For it's the star that guides our journey
And leads us safely home.

Clay Harrison

The Journey

Each soul is on a journey,
Through the vestiges of time,

In keeping with God's holy plan,
Gleaning the sublime,

Grace of His eternal love,
Where peace and wisdom stay,

He guides and gently leads us,
Each step along the way.

Colette Fedor

A Prayer

Tell me what to do, Lord –
Sometimes I'm at a loss.
I make mountains out of mole hills,
Complain about my cross.

Tell me what to do today,
Prompt me with what to say.
Fill me with your Spirit,
Teach me how to pray.

Helen Parker

*You have made known to
me the paths of life; You
will fill me with joy in
Your presence.*
Acts 2:28

The Holy Spirit's Touch

Lord, someone's having heartache
And lost the will to go on –
Her spirit is in turmoil
And her zest for life is gone.

She smiles on the outside
But hides bitter tears inside –
She needs to feel Your presence, God,
And to know You're by her side.

So whisper words of comfort,
Let her feel Your holy touch;
Still the raging storm within –
Let her know You love so much.

Help her "be still and know" You're God
And to listen for Your voice;
Speak to her with words of love
So that she's left with no choice…

But to turn her eyes upward
And let You so fill her soul,
That praising and serving You
Will be her ultimate goal.

Lord, when we give our all to You,
Yes, even our emotions –
We learn to lean on You, and
We're filled with such devotion…

That loving You replaces
All the sad tears that we've shed,
And in their place we find ourselves
Crying tears of joy instead.

You can turn despair to joy –
For that we praise Your name!
Your Holy Spirit takes hold…
And we are never the same!

Denise A. DeWald

Teach me wisdom and knowledge, for in Your commands I trust.
Psalm 119:66

Lessons

There are many lessons
To be learned each day;
We can grow in wisdom
On our earthly way –
And learn to be much kinder,
Sincere and loving, too,
Showing true compassion
In all the things we do –
Lessons can be varied;
There are many to be sure,
Ones that tell of virtue
In being good and pure –
Often we don't heed them,
The lessons that come by,
But with great desire,
We can daily try.

Virginia Borman Grimmer

*Lord, do not withhold Your
compassion from me; may
Your enduring kindness
ever preserve me.*
Psalm 40:12

Wintertime

Wintertime is a special time
To show how much God cares,
By sending snow to cover things
So they won't look so bare.

He clothes the trees that have no leaves;
He makes them look brand new.
And diamonds seem to sparkle
With sun rays shining through.

He seems to give our special earth
Some extra time to rest,
So springtime can replace it
And birds can build their nests.

God gives the rivers time to rest
Frozen deep with ice and snow,
Just waiting for the Spring to come
So they again can flow.

Yes, wintertime is a special time
To show how much we care,
By taking time to spend with God
His blessings we all share.

Bonnie J. Knapp

My soul, be at rest in God alone,
from whom comes my hope.
Psalm 62:6

May the God of hope fill you with all joy and peace in believing, so that you may abound in hope by the power of the Holy Spirit.
Romans 15:13

Winter

Winter puts the earth to sleep;
She tucks it snugly in bed,
A soft snowflake-blanket laid
So gently about its head.
The sights and sounds of Nature
Are now hushed in Winter's white,
And creating dreams in peace
Of the springtime, warm and bright.
Winter brings us God's message
To slow down and rest awhile,
And contemplate His blessings,
Like dear loved ones, hugs and smiles.

Steven Michael Schumacher

Then the Lord looked
upon the earth, and filled
it with His blessings.
Sirach 16:27

The Rocky Road

There's a road that leads to Heaven
And it takes me to our Lord.
The stumbling blocks are many
And, at times, the traveling is hard.
If this road was smooth and clear
And remained perilous free,
I could not advance in wisdom –
There would be no growth for me.
Every rock and every pebble
Has a purpose on this road.
They give me strength and courage
And will help to make me bold.

Every time I tend to stumble
And might fall upon my face,
I know that God will pick me up
With His gentle, loving grace.
When, at last, my journey is over
And I finally reach my road's end,
I will be filled with love and gratitude –
There will be no more twists and bends.

Shirley Hile Powell

Heavenly Father

Oh merciful God, so gentle and kind,
So often I'm troubled, so much on my mind.
My cares I promised to leave at Your feet
But be as it may, I am humanly weak.

If You loan me tomorrow, I'll try harder to please.
I'll ask for direction down on my knees.
Lord, let Your mercy sustain me each day.
Teach me compassion for others, I pray.

Helen Parker

Answer me, Lord, in Your
generous love; in Your great
mercy turn to me.
Psalm 69:17